Anne
Fine

Keep It in the Family

PENGUIN BOOKS

PENGUIN BOOKS

Published by the Penguin Group
Penguin Books Ltd, 27 Wrights Lane, London w8 5tz, England
Penguin Books USA Inc., 375 Hudson Street, New York, New York 10014, USA
Penguin Books Australia Ltd, Ringwood, Victoria, Australia
Penguin Books Canada Ltd, 10 Alcorn Avenue, Toronto, Ontario, Canada m4v 3b2
Penguin Books (NZ) Ltd, 182–190 Wairau Road, Auckland 10, New Zealand

Penguin Books Ltd, Registered Offices: Harmondsworth, Middlesex, England

'William Darling' was first published in *Shark and Chips and Other Stories*
published in Puffin Books 1992; 'You Don't Look Very Poorly' was first
published in *The Puffin Book of Funny Stories* (Ed. Helen Cresswell) by Viking
1992 and in Puffin Books 1993; 'Fight the Good Fight' was first published in
Streets Ahead (Ed. Valerie Bierman) by Methuen Children's Books 1989

This collection published in Penguin Books 1996
3 5 7 9 10 8 6 4

Copyright © Anne Fine, 1989, 1992 and 1996
All rights reserved

The moral right of the author has been asserted

Set in 12.5/14.5pt Bembo Monotype
Typeset by Datix International Limited, Bungay, Suffolk
Printed in England by Clays Ltd, St Ives plc

Contents

William Darling

IT isn't even my real name, that's what gets me. I can see that if I'd been *born* with a name like William Darling, if it was written in great curly letters across my *birth* certificate or something, then I might have to put up with it. But it isn't even my proper name!

I had trouble from my first day at school. I was in more fights than anyone Mrs Hurd could remember, and she'd been teaching twenty years. It took weeks for some of the people in my class to realize that, when they sidled up and whispered, 'Hello, William Darling,' I was going to turn round and biff them. I don't like being teased myself, and I certainly don't like to hear people teasing my father.

Mind you, it's his own fault. He started it off. I'm sure he didn't mean to cause me any trouble. It just worked out that way. You see, my father's *terribly* old. His hair's all silver, he gets arthritis in damp weather, and he uses huge spotted cotton handkerchiefs, not paper tissues, to blow his nose when he gets a cold. (He makes the most extraordinary trumpeting noise. People look round.) He had another family, all grown up before he even *thought* of marrying my mother and starting on me. They drop in every now and again, and it's so odd to think that they're my half-brothers. They look old enough to be my father. And my father looks old enough to be my grandpa.

And he's old-fashioned, too. He likes things like starched sheets and fountain pens you fill from glass ink bottles, and mealtimes so late that Mum and I have practically starved to death before the food's even on the table.

And he calls me William Darling.

He doesn't mean anything by it, I know. He doesn't *want* to make my life difficult. It's just he's too set in his ways to change.

2   He should have grown up at Wallisdean

Primary School. He'd know a lot better then! He'd know that it's quite all right if your mother leans over the school fence and calls out, 'Hurry up, darling!' Nobody thinks twice about it. Nobody even seems to *hear*. But if your father does it, you're in big trouble – or a lot of fights.

Me, I was in a lot of fights. It took weeks before my father could stroll along to school with me in the morning and hand me my lunchbox, saying, 'There you are, darling,' without great choruses of sniggers breaking out all around me. I had to get tough with Melissa Halestrap for eight days in a row before she learned to stop lifting my coat off its hook at the end of the day and handing it to me with a really good imitation of my father's voice: 'Come along, William Darling. Button up. Freezy cold outside!'

No, it wasn't easy. I had to work at things at Wallisdean Primary. But I managed. And in the end I was perfectly satisfied and happy (and even

Mrs Hurd admitted to my mum at the jumble sale in aid of the school roof that I'd stopped all that frightful fighting, and matured a lot). Then, suddenly, one day, the bombshell dropped.

'And when you move on to your next school in September . . .'

That's all Mrs Hurd said. (What I mean is, I was so shocked I didn't listen to the rest.) I'm not *stupid*. I knew I was in the school's oldest class. I knew we moved on. So I must have *realized* it was our last term at Wallisdean. It's just I hadn't realized how soon the change was. And, worse, it suddenly struck me that, just as I'd finally persuaded everybody in this school that it was a really bad idea to try and get away with calling me William Darling, I'd have to start all over again somewhere else.

And it would be even harder than before. Everyone would be older, and the older you get, the sillier William Darling sounds to you. And though I didn't know exactly what sort of teasing you'd get in the new school, I felt pretty sure of one thing: it would be worse.

I fretted about it, on and off, for the whole of the last two weeks of the term. And through the start of the summer holidays. Then, when I saw that worrying was spoiling everything, I reckoned I'd try tackling the matter head on. I thought it would be best.

'Please,' I said to my father. 'Since I'm starting at a new school, will you try to get out of the habit of calling me William Darling?'

He lowered his *Financial Times* and peered at me over it through the gold-rimmed half-moon spectacles he wears three-quarters of the way down his nose.

'Quite understand,' he told me. 'No problem, sweetheart.'

You can see why I wasn't optimistic. William Sweetheart is no better. And when, by the end of the week, he'd called me pumpkin, poppet, 5 lambkin and muffin in his attempts to avoid the dreaded word, I just gave up.

Only three weeks to go. Have to try something else.

Sulking. I'd try sulking. I wouldn't answer him. If he called me William Darling, I'd go all fish-faced, and refuse to respond.

It didn't work, of course. He hates me being miserable. He hovered over me the entire week. 'What's the matter? Something up? Do tell. Oh, what a gloomy bird you are, darling!'

No luck there, then. And only two weeks to go. I was getting so desperate I thought I'd try bribery. I've found that bribery often works when all else fails.

'If I weed the whole garden,' I wheedled. 'Properly. Front *and* back. *And* down the side behind the garage. *And* along the verge –'

His spoon drifted to a halt halfway between his breakfast bowl of stewed prunes and his open 6 mouth. One bushy silver eyebrow shot up. I thought he might be going to have a heart attack.

'If I do all that, will you stop calling me William Darling?'

'Of *course* I will, William, darling!'

'Starting right *now*!'

'Yes, d –' He practically had to choke it back with the stewed prunes. 'Yes, William.' He practised it to himself sternly, several times, in between mouthfuls. 'Yes, William. Thank you, William. Oh, really, William? Quite so, William. Quite so.'

I left him chuntering, and strode out determinedly to the toolshed. I worked the whole day. I never stopped, except when Mum brought out a plate of sandwiches and shared them with me on the steps, admiring all the work I'd done, and helping me replant all the marigolds I'd pulled out of the ground by mistake.

At half-past five I finished the very last square 7

millimetre of the verge. I waved triumphantly to Mum, and she went to fetch him.

They came back arm in arm. They strolled round the garden together as if the place were owned by the National Trust, praising everything, and gasping at how tidy it looked. Then he turned round and pressed a brand-new, shiny ten-pence piece into my hand. (He often does this. He's so old that he thinks ten pence is a fortune. It's one of the worst things about marrying someone a lot older than yourself, Mum says. You spend a fiver, and they think you're wicked.)

'Thank you,' I said, and put the coin in my pocket.

'Don't lose it,' he warned me.

Don't lose it! I get ten of them every week for pocket money. He must know that. But he's in the habit of keeping shiny coins he comes across in a special pocket in his waistcoat, ready to press them on the deserving, and he's too old to bother to change. So I held my tongue.

Pity he didn't.

'Splendid!' he said, waving to indicate my handiwork. 'You've done a beautiful job, William, darling!'

Mum tried to save the day. She spun him round and started pointing out how well the sweet peas were growing up the wall. But I was desperate. I'd slaved all day, and I'd got nowhere. I couldn't help it. I just lost my temper. Hurling the hoe down on the lawn, I yelled at him that I'd spent the *whole day* working because we'd made a *deal*, he'd *promised* me, and what happens? What's the very first thing he says? William Darling!

I threw my arms out, and wailed dramatically, 'What can I *do*? I'm not a baby any more! You've got to get out of the habit of calling me William Darling!'

It's always a bad move, losing your temper in front of anyone over fifty-five. They're old enough to think it's disgraceful. 9

'Listen to me, William,' he said. 'Manners like that simply will not do. I am extremely sorry that, so soon after our little agreement, the word happened to slip out. But tantrums are quite inexcusable. Pick up that hoe.'

I picked up that hoe.

'And kindly apologize to your mother.'

I muttered something that might, or might not, have been 'Sorry, Mum'. She didn't mind. She understood perfectly well how ratty I was getting about the whole business. *She* knew I wasn't a baby any more. *She* understood that things would be very different at the new school.

And maybe that's the reason she fixed up that arrangement the next day. Maybe that's why she made a special point of making my father take me into town shopping. 'He needs an awful lot of new stuff,' she said. 'You can take him.'

'Me? Why *me*?' (He hates shopping. He says the assistants are 'too big for their boots' and don't know the first thing about what they're selling. He nearly had a stroke last year when the girl in Woolies paused in the act of snipping the elastic thread Mum was buying, and asked how many centimetres there were in a metre. Mum pretends it was the girl's shocking mathematics that so upset him. But I know better. I know it was the fact that, until then, he hadn't realized yards, feet and inches have gone.)

'You have to take him,' Mum insisted. 'Because I'll be at work. And you're retired.'

No arguing with that. He had to take me.

He didn't enjoy it. First we went into Brierleys to buy an electronic calculator – not any old cheap one for beginners, but the sort my new school recommends, the Fz 753xb, which does all manner of fancy things I certainly hope I'll never need.

'Bit sophisticated, isn't it?' he said, inspecting the price sticker with even more interest than the calculator itself. 'For a child.'

The shop girl gave him a pretty cool look.

'Pretty sophisticated maths they do at this young man's age,' she retorted.

He looked around for the young man, and was a bit put out just to see me.

'Hrrrumph,' he said. But he wrote out the cheque, and signed it with his extraordinary flourish.

Then we went to Skinners to buy football boots. As soon as they found a pair that fitted me, he handed over the cheque he'd been filling out while I was lacing up.

'Eight pounds, twenty,' he said.

She shook her head and handed the cheque back to him with the neatly written bill.

'Twelve pounds, ten pence,' she corrected him. 'Your boy is in the large foot range now.'

Without saying a word, he tore the first cheque into tiny pieces. Then, still without speaking, he wrote out another.

12   He was in quite a mood by the time we

reached Hilliards to buy my new blazer. He strode straight over to the rack which had the smallest sizes hanging from it, and had to be steered to the taller rack behind, where all the larger (and more expensive) ones hung.

'Bit pricey,' he complained.

'Wait till he shoots up,' said the shop assistant. 'He'll grow out of a blazer a week!'

My father looked horrified. When he wrote the cheque, his hand was trembling. It can't be easy for a man who still thinks that ten pence is wealth.

He claimed that he needed some time to recover.

'Bills, bills, bills!' he groused. 'Let's go and have a cup of tea while the feeling returns to my cheque-signing fingers.'

He chose the same old teashop we've gone to for years. (Mum says they bought their first high chair for me.) We took our usual table, and my father gave the usual order to the new summer waitress.

13

'One lightly buttered toasted teacake, and a Balloon Special.'

(Maybe I should tell you that, with a Balloon Special, you get three flavours of ice-cream, and a big red balloon tied to the back of your chair.)

The waitress gave me a suspicious look.

'He looks a bit old for a Balloon Special,' she said. 'It's only supposed to be for sevens and under.' (She was so new, she still remembered the rules.)

'Really?' said my father frostily. 'Then *two* lightly buttered toasted teacakes.'

I didn't argue. I suddenly reckoned I understood why Mum had been so keen to send us off together. She wanted him to realize for himself I wasn't a baby any longer. I did hard maths. I had big feet. If I'd grown out of big red balloons and into teacakes, maybe I'd also grown out of being called William Darling.

I wasn't his darling right now, that was for

sure. He was flicking back through the chequebook.

'Bills, bills, bills!' he grumbled. 'You're costing me a fortune. I ought to call you "bill"!'

The waitress sailed over with the teacakes.

'One for me,' said my father. 'And one for "bill" here.'

She laid the teacakes down without so much as a flicker of her eyebrows. She obviously thought what he said sounded perfectly normal.

And so it did, of course – bill-William-Bill!

I couldn't believe my luck. The joke amused him so much, he kept it up all the way home: 'Tired, bill?' and all through the evening: 'Nice mug of hot chocolate, bill?' and at bedtime: 'Cleaned your teeth, bill?' The joke ran for *weeks*. Sometimes I worried that he might be on the verge of finding it boring, but I'd just leave out my calculator, or my blazer, or my new football boots, and he'd be off again: 'Getting ready for school, bill?'

And, to my amazement, the joke was still making him chuckle right through the last days of the holiday, and the parents' evening. Grinning, my father introduced me to my new form teacher.

'This is my bill,' he said.

Mr Henry looked at me.

'Hello, Bill.'

That was all he said!

And it went on that way. I couldn't believe my good fortune was holding. When I walked in the classroom on the first morning, all Mr Henry said was, 'Here, Bill. These books are for you,' and by break everybody just called me Bill as if I'd never in my life been William Darling.

I stayed Bill all through lunch, and all afternoon. I stayed Bill all week – no fuss, no fights. Mrs Hurd would have been astonished. She wouldn't have known me. I worried sometimes, quite a lot, because I knew I couldn't keep my father away from the school grounds for ever, but then I'd put the anxiety out of my mind, and just enjoy things.

And then, this afternoon, it finally happened. Our class was playing football on the pitch, when suddenly I caught sight of my father's straw boater sailing along on the other side of the school hedge. I kept my head down, dreading the moment I just *knew* was coming the instant he reached the gap at the gate, glanced in, and saw me. Chills ran down my spine. My knees were shaking. Did I have time to run off the pitch?

Too late! Over the gate I heard his clear, clear voice.

'Go for it, William, darling! Boot that ball!'

The football was sailing down towards me, head on. Swinging my foot back, I booted it as hard as I could, *really* hard, as if to let the teasers know, right from the very start, what I could do.

The ball flew down the pitch in a perfect arc.

Then I looked round. No teasers? Mr Henry

called out, 'Well done, Bill!' as he puffed past, but no one else was paying the slightest attention. No one was even looking my way. They'd all gone haring up the field after the ball, and I suddenly realized that no one had, even for a single moment, connected me with that silvery-haired (and probably confused) old gentleman who yelled encouragement over the fence, and then strolled on.

William Darling? No. No William Darling in this game, I'm afraid. Me? Oh, my name's Bill.

You Don't Look Very Poorly

ADAPTED FROM *CRUMMY MUMMY AND ME*

This was the first of what turned out to be several stories about Minna and her unusual family.

YOU don't exactly *ask* to get sick, do you? I mean, you don't go round *inviting* germs and viruses to move in and do their worst to your body. You don't actually *apply* for trembling legs and feeling shivery, and a head that's had a miniature steel band practising for a carnival in it all night.

And if you should happen to mention to your own mother that you feel absolutely terrible, you would expect a bit of sympathy, wouldn't you?

I wouldn't. Not any more.

'You don't *look* very poorly.'

That's what she said. And she said it suspiciously, too, as if I was one of those people who's 19 always making excuses to stay off school and spend the day wrapped in a downie on the sofa watching *Bagpuss* and *Playschool* and *Pebble Mill at One.*

'Well, I feel absolutely rotten.'

'You don't look it.'

'I'm sorry!' I snapped. (I was getting pretty cross.) 'Sorry I can't manage a bright-green face for you! Or purple spots on my belly! Or all my hair falling out! But I feel rotten just the same!'

And I burst into tears.

(Now that's not like me.)

'Now that's not like you,' said Mum, sounding sympathetic at last. 'You must be a little bit off today.'

'I am not *off*,' I snarled through my tears. 'I'm not leftover milk. Or rotten fish.'

'There, there,' Mum soothed. 'Don't fret, Minna. Don't get upset. You just hop straight back up those stairs like a good poppet, and in a minute I'll bring something nice up on a tray, and you can have a quiet day in bed, with Mum looking after you until you feel better.'

That was a bit more like it, as I think you'll agree. So I stopped snivelling and went back to bed. I didn't exactly hop straight back up those stairs because I was feeling so crummy and weak I could barely drag myself up hanging on to the banisters; but I got up somehow, and put on my dressing-gown and buttoned it right up to the top to keep my chest warm, and plumped up my pillows so I could sit comfortably, and switched on my little plastic frog reading-lamp, and folded my hands in my lap, and I waited.

And I waited.

And I waited.

(In case you're wondering, I was waiting for Mum to bring me up something nice on a tray and look after me until I felt better.)

She never came.

Oh, I'm sure that she *meant* to come. I'm sure she had every intention of coming. I'm sure it 21 wasn't her fault the milkman came and needed paying, and it took time to work out what she owed because he'd been away for two weeks on his holiday in Torremolinos.

And I'm sure it wasn't Mum's fault that he took the opportunity to park his crate of bottles down on the doorstep and tell her all about the way some sneaky people always bagged the best pool-loungers by creeping down at dead of night and dropping their swimming towels over them; and how his wife's knees burned and peeled but none of the rest of her, even though all of her was out in the sun for the same amount of time; and how his daughter Meryl came home to her job at the Halifax with a broken heart because of some fellow called Miguel Angel Gippini Lopez de Rego, who danced like a fury but turned out to be engaged to a Spanish girl working in Barcelona.

Oh, it wasn't Mum's fault that she had to listen
to all that before she could get away to bring me

up something nice on a tray and look after me until I was better. But I could hear them talking clearly enough on the doorstep. And I don't actually recall hearing her say firmly but politely: 'Excuse me, Mr Hooper, but Minna's in bed feeling terrible, and I must get back upstairs, so I'll listen to all the rest tomorrow.' I heard quite a bit; but I didn't hear that.

As soon as the milkman had chinked off next door, I thought I heard Mum making for the bottom of the stairs. But she never got there.

'YeeeeooooowwwwwwaaaaaAAAAAAAAAA-EEEEEWWW!'

You guessed it. My baby sister woke up.

And I suppose it wasn't Mum's fault that Miranda needed her nappy changing. And that there weren't any dry ones because we don't have a tumble-drier and it had been raining for three solid days. And Mum had forgotten to pick up another packet of disposables last time she practically *swam* down to the shops. 23

So Mum decided the simplest thing would be to park Miranda in the playpen where little accidents don't matter. It wasn't her fault it took for ever to drag it out of the cupboard because she had dumped my sledge, and the dress-up box, and all the empty jars she's saving for Gran right in front of it. Or that she had to fetch the damp nappies off the line and drape them over the rack in the kitchen.

And I suppose it's understandable that while she was shaking out the damp nappies, she should glance out of the window at the grey skies and think about nipping down to the launderette with the rest of the washing and handing it to Mrs Hajee to do in the machines, since it really didn't look as if it would ever stop raining.

So I suppose it does make sense that the very next thing I heard on my quiet day in bed was Mum bellowing up the stairs: 'Minna! *Minna!* Look after the baby for a few minutes, will you, while I nip down to the launderette? She's perfectly happy in her playpen with her toys. Just come down if she starts to squawk.'

Fine. Lovely. Sure. Here am I, feeling really terrible and looking forward to something nice on a tray and being looked after until I feel better, and suddenly I'm looking after the baby! Fine. Lovely. Sure.

To be quite fair to Mum, she didn't stay out any longer than was absolutely necessary. There was the launderette, of course. And then she had to get the disposable nappies or Miranda would have had to spend the whole morning sitting on her cold bottom in the playpen, waiting for the ones in the kitchen to dry. And while she was in the supermarket she did pick up bread, and a quarter of sliced ham, and a few oranges and a couple of other things, making too many to get through the quick checkout. And there were really long queues at all the others because it was pension-day morning. And she did just pop into the newsagent's on her way home as well. And, yes, she did stop on the corner for a second, but that was just to be polite to the Lollipop Lady who told her that, whatever it was I'd got, there was a lot of it about, and Mum ought to be really careful or she'd come down with it as well.

And then she came straight home. She *says* she was out for no more than five minutes at the very most. But I've a watch, so I know better.

Then, at last, she came up to my room. She had Miranda tucked under one arm, all bare bottom and wriggles, and she was carrying a tray really high in the air, practically above her head, so my sister couldn't upset it with all her flailing arms and legs. It was so high I couldn't see what was on it from the bed.

'I don't know how these nurses do it,' said Mum. 'They should have medals pinned on their chests, not watches.'

I looked at mine. It was exactly half-past ten.
26 (I fell sick at 8.23.)

'If you were a nurse,' I said, 'you would have got the sack two hours ago.'

'I'd like to see you do any better,' she snapped back, sharpish.

'I bet I would,' I told her. 'I bet if *you* were sick, it wouldn't take *me* two whole hours to bring you something nice on a tray.'

'I should wait till you see what there is on the tray before you start grumbling,' Mum warned. And then she lowered it on to the bed in front of me.

And there was a cup of very milky coffee with bubbles on top in my favourite fat china bear mug, and a huge orange cut into the thinnest possible circular slices, just how I like it when I want to nibble at the peel as well. And a chocolate-biscuit bar and the latest *Beano* and *Dandy*, and a pack of twenty brand-new fine-tipped felt pens.

I felt dead guilty for being so grumpy.

'I'm sorry I said you'd get the sack as a nurse.' 27

'Oh, that's all right,' Mum answered cheerfully. She flipped Miranda over and put a nappy on her before there was trouble and even more laundry. 'It's a well-known fact that it's even harder to be a good patient than a good nurse.'

'Is that true?'

'Certainly.'

And then, with my baby sister safe at last, Mum sat down on my bed and took a break.

I thought about what she said quite a lot while I was getting better. As I sipped my coffee, and nibbled my orange circles, and read my *Beano*, and made my chocolate biscuit last as long as I could while I was drawing with my brand-new felt pens, I wondered what sort of patient Mum would make. She isn't famous in this house for long-suffering meekness or sunny patience.

And I wondered what sort of nurse I'd make — sensitive, deft, unflappable, efficient . . .

28   I'd no idea I would find out so soon.

It was only two days later, on Saturday morning, that Mum leaned over the banisters and called down: 'Minna, I feel just awful. Awful.'

'You don't *look* very poorly.'

(I didn't mean it that way. It just popped out.)

You'd have thought I was trying to suggest she was faking.

'I may not *look* it, but I *am*,' she snapped. 'I feel as if I've been left out all night in the rain, and my bones have gone soggy, and hundreds of spiteful little men with steel boots are holding a stamping competition in my brain.'

Personally, even without the Lollipop Lady saying there was a lot of it about, I would have recognized the symptoms at once.

I was determined to show Mum what proper nursing ought to be.

'You go straight back to bed,' I ordered. 'I'll take care of you, and everything else. You tuck yourself in comfortably, and I'll bring up something nice on a tray.'

Mum swayed a little against the banisters. She did look pale.

'You are an angel, Minna,' she said faintly. And wrapping her shiny black skull-and-crossbones dressing-gown more closely around her string-vest nightie, she staggered back into the bedroom.

I don't have to tell you about my plan, do I? You'll already have guessed. Yes, I was going to rush back into the kitchen and spread a tray with lovely, tempting treats for an invalid's breakfast – treats like a cup of tea made just the way Mum really likes it, golden-pale, not that lovely, thick, murky, dark sludge favoured by me and Gran. (We joke that Mum's tea is too weak to crawl out of the pot.) And I was going to pick a tiny posy of flowers from the garden, and arrange them in one of the pretty china egg cups.

And I was going to bring the tray up without delay.

Guess what went wrong first. No, don't

bother. I'll tell you. First, I locked myself out. Honestly. Me, Minna. The only one in the house who *never* does it. I did it. I was so keen to get my tray arranged that I stepped out of the back door into the garden to find the flowers without checking the latch.

Clunk!

The moment I heard the door close behind me, I realized. I could have kicked myself in the shins. I picked my way around to the front, just on the off-chance that the front door was unlocked. But I knew it wouldn't be, and of course it wasn't.

I stood there, thinking. I had two choices. I could ring the doorbell and drag poor, shaking, deathly pale Mum from her bed of sickness and down the stairs to let me in; or I could slip next door to old Mrs Pitopoulos, ring her bell instead, and ask to borrow the spare key to our house she keeps for emergencies in an old cocoa tin under her sink.

I knew which a good nurse would do. I went next door and rang the bell.

No answer.

I rang again.

Still no answer.

Suddenly I noticed a faint scrabbling overhead. I looked up, and there was Mrs Pitopoulos in her quilted dressing-gown, fighting the stiff window-catch with her arthritic fingers.

She couldn't budge it, so she just beckoned me inside the house.

I tried the front door. It was locked. I went round the back, and that door opened. I picked my way through the furry sea of all her pet cats rubbing their arched backs against my legs, so pleased to see me, and went upstairs.

Mrs Pitopoulos was sitting on the edge of her bed. Her face looked like a wrinkled sack, and her wig was all crooked.

'You look very poorly,' I told her.

I couldn't help it. It just popped out.

'Oh, Minna,' she said. 'I feel terrible, terrible. My legs are rubber, and there are red-hot nails in my head.'

'I've had that,' I said. 'Mum's got it now. The Lollipop Lady says that there's lots of it about.'

When she heard this, Mrs Pitopoulos began to look distinctly better. Maybe when you're that age and you get sick, you think whatever it is has come to get you. At any rate, she tugged her wig round on her head, and even the wrinkles seemed to flatten out a bit.

'Minna,' she said. 'Would you do me a great favour, and feed my hungry cats?'

'What about you?' I said. 'Have you had anything this morning?'

'Oh I'm not hungry,' Mrs Pitopoulos declared.

But then she cocked her head on one side, and wondered about it. And then she added: 'Maybe I do feel just a little bit peckish. Yesterday my sister brought me all these lovely things: new-laid brown speckled eggs and home-made bread and a tiny pot of fresh strawberry jam. But what I'd really like is . . .' (Her eyes were gleaming, and she looked miles better.) 'What I'd really like is a bowl of Heinz tomato soup with bits of white bread floating on the top.'

Even I can cook that.

And so I did. And fed her cats. And she was so pleased when I brought the soup up to her on a tray that she pressed on me all the little gifts her sister had brought round the day before: the new-laid brown speckled eggs and home-made bread and tiny pot of fresh strawberry jam – oh, and the door key of course.

Mum was astonished when I brought the tray up. I thought she must have been asleep. She looked as if she had been dozing. She heaved herself upright against the pillows, and I laid the tray down on her knees.

'Minna!' she cried. 'Oh, how lovely! Look at the flowers!'

'Wait till you've tasted the food,' I said.

I could tell that she didn't really feel much like eating. But she was determined not to hurt my feelings, so she reached out and took one of the strips of hot buttered toast made from the home-made bread.

She nibbled the crust politely.

'Delicious,' she said. And then, 'Mmm. *Delicious.*'

She couldn't help dipping the next strip of toast into the new-laid brown speckled soft-boiled egg.

'Mmmm!' she cried. 'This is *wonderful.*'

After the egg was eaten, she still had two strips of toast left. She spread one with the fresh strawberry jam, and off she went again.

'Mmmm! *Marvellous!*'

She went into raptures over the golden-pale tea. (I reckoned I'd have a battle ever forcing her back to medium-brown, when she felt well again.) And then she leaned back against the pillows, smiling.

She looked a lot better.

'I'll bring you some more, if you'd like it,' I offered.

'You are the *very best nurse*,' Mum declared. 'You managed all this, and so quickly too!'

Now I was sure she'd been dozing. I'd taken *ages*.

'You're the *very best patient*,' I returned the compliment. 'You don't notice what's going on, or how long it takes!'

'Silly,' she said, and snuggled back under the bedcovers.

I think she must have thought I was joking.

Fight the Good Fight

Both my daughters hate *the smell of cigarette smoke.
(Like my heroine's granny, I've a soft spot for it
myself.) I was used to hearing them grumble about
it each time they came home from school on the city
bus, and wrote this story to show that I was really on
their side.*

*Authors often write to try to alter something in
society. So we can have mixed feelings when things
change, in case our work looks a little out of date. But
the best part of us wants to cheer that the world can
change so much so quickly. So enjoy a little bit of
history!*

'I've heard of fighting the good fight,' the bus
driver says to me almost every morning when I
get off, 'but you are really weird.' He shakes his
head. 'Really weird.'

He's quite wrong. I'm perfectly *normal*. There's
nothing *wrong* with me. I'm probably about the 37

same age as you. I'm probably about as clever, and I can take a joke, just like you. The only thing different about me is that I hate cigarette smoke. I just can't stand it. I think it stinks.

It's only the smell of it I hate. I quite like the way it looks. I used to love sitting on my mum's knee, watching the wispy streams of fine blue smoke float up from her fag ends (before I frightened her into giving up with all my talk of 'coughin' nails'). I liked the way that, when she moved, or laughed, or waved her hand as she was talking, the smoke would twist and wind on its way up to the ceiling, and you could blow on it gently, till it drifted into great billowing circles.

And I liked watching my dad smoke his pipe, too (before he threw it in the rubbish after I saw a smoker's lungs on telly, all brown and kippery, and burst into tears). I liked the way he puffed out huge silvery-blue clouds, and smacked his lips, making little putt-putt-putt noises, whenever he thought it might be going out. He was an ace pipe-smoker, my dad — a real professional. He once kept it going all the way home from my granny's in a rainstorm.

Granny's the only one of my relations who smokes now (when she can stop coughing long enough to take a good puff). But since I only see her every other Saturday, I don't really mind.

What I mind is the bus.

My bus, the number 14, runs from one end of the city to the other. It's only a single decker, so in the mornings it gets terribly crowded, partly with people like me going to school, and partly with adults on their way to work. By the time the bus reaches my stop, Railton Dyke End, at ten past eight, there's hardly ever any seats left. I usually have to stand for fifteen minutes, till I get off at the end of Great Barr Street. And the bus is sometimes so crowded I get pushed further and further down the gangway.

And that's the problem. That's why the bus driver thinks I'm so weird. I can't stand moving further down the gangway. The front half of the bus is fine by me. It's all non-smoking, with little red stickers saying so on the windows, and nothing but clean bright-green peppermint wrappers stuffed in the ashtrays, and even a sign on the glass pane behind the driver's back that says *Have a heart – Stop smoking now.* But the back of the bus is disgusting. It's all grey-faced men and women wheezing and coughing and spluttering out clouds of their filthy-smelling grey smoke, and flicking their dirty ash flakes on one another's clothing, and leaving their fag ends smouldering in the overflowing ashtrays, and trampling their nasty little soggy yellow stubs on the floor in their hurry to get off the bus at the right stop, and light up another.

It's horrible. I hate it. I wouldn't mind so much if the smell stayed down their end with them, and you could turn your back on the whole revolting spectacle and just pretend it wasn't there. But not only does stale smoke drift up to our end, but sometimes when the bus gets really crowded, the driver even tries to force you to move further along and stand at the filthy end, stop after stop, while the vile smell seeps into your clothes and your hair, and even your skin.

'Move along inside. Move down the bus, *please*. You, too.' (He means me.)

'Did you hear what the driver said, little girl? Make room. Move along a bit.'

I cling desperately to the rail of the last pair of non-smoking seats.

'Sorry, I can't move down any further. That's the smoking end, and I don't smoke.'

Sometimes people glare. Sometimes they mutter. But, mostly, they just stare at me as if I were bonkers.

And I'm not. As I said at the start, I am a perfectly normal person. There's nothing weird about preferring halfway reasonable air to standing over some stranger's personal miniature chemical refinery, breathing in the waste fumes. 41

I don't see why I should be forced to move down the bus.

'You clog up my gangway every morning,' the bus driver complains when I force my way up to the very front, to get off. 'You ought to be more co-operative.'

I don't see why. I wouldn't co-operate with putting my head in a noose. I wouldn't co-operate with throwing myself out of a helicopter without a parachute. I don't see why I should co-operate with getting my lungs black.

But when I tell him so as he slows down at the corner of the street that leads to my school, he gets all snappy with me.

'You should go through the proper channels,' he tells me. 'You should stop making trouble on my bus.'

But I'd tried proper channels. Proper channels were perfectly useless, I can tell you. I got my mother to write a letter to the bus company, and all she got back was some very polite rubbish about 'fully appreciating her point of view', but 'having to consider the feelings of the other passengers'.

Well, what about my feelings? Don't they count? I catch the bus every single morning we have school. I have for years. That's over two hundred times a year. That's over a thousand bus rides *already*. I'd have to be a real drip not to fight back. So, over the years, I have developed my own private methods of making people stub their cigarettes out on the bus. (That's what the driver means by 'making trouble'.)

My first method is the best. It works the quickest, especially on motherly women with lots of shopping bags who are having their first quiet fag of the morning. Just as my victim lights up and leans back, sighing with pleasure, I lean towards her and, tugging a grubby old paper tissue out of my pocket, I start to snivel. If my victim doesn't notice, I sob a bit, quietly, and start my shoulders heaving up and down. I try to get real tears rolling down my cheeks, but that only tends to work if I get in the cigarette's slipstream.

After less than a minute the victim always asks kindly: 'Are you crying, little girl? What's the matter?'

'Nothing.'

I wipe my nose on the back of my hand, but sweetly, like a small child in a family film, not disgustingly, like Gareth Chatterton in primary four.

The victim leans forward and whispers: 'Come on, dear. You can tell me. Are you hurt?'

I shake my head.

'In trouble?'

'No-oo.'

'Is anyone at school picking on you?'

'No,' I say. 'It's not that. It's –' I make my voice tremble. And then I hesitate, so she has to ask again.

'What is it, dear?'

44　　Then I look her straight in the eye.

'It's my aunty,' I say. 'She used to smoke, too. The same brand as you. But now she's got —' I pause, and watch the cigarette as it burns away between her fingers. Then, while the little word I'm *not* saying rings an alarm bell in my victim's brain, I finish up delicately: 'Well, she's very ill. She can hardly breathe now.'

At this point the victim always stubs out her fag, and looks thoughtfully at the little cardboard packet in her hand. I don't feel guilty. Why should I? Better she's my victim than the cigarette's, after all. And when it comes to getting a bit of fresh air on our bus, every quick stub-out helps.

I used this method a lot in the beginning. It worked a treat. The only problem was that the bus tends to carry the same passengers, day after day, so after a week or two only new passengers bothered to ask me why I was so unhappy.

So I moved on to method number two.

'I can smell fire!'

'Fire?'

'Fire!'

Everyone holds their fags up a little bit higher, and inspects them carefully. Then they inspect the folds in their clothing, and peer down between the bags and briefcases on the floor, to see if a burning cigarette has set something smouldering.

'Really. I can smell something burning. Can't you smell it? It's very strong.'

'It's just the cigarette smoke, dear.'

'Oh, no,' I argue. 'It couldn't just be cigarette smoke. It smells *disgusting*, and it's getting *worse*.'

One by one, people at the back are getting nervous and stubbing out their cigarettes just that little bit early.

'I can still smell it. I'm sure everyone can. There is a definite smell of burning. It's terribly strong, and very nasty.'

Sometimes I can get every single passenger at the back of the bus neatly stubbed out before we even reach the Safeway at the bottom of Dean Bank.

Then there's method number three. That's when I double over in a coughing fit, and make my face go pink, then red, then blue if it isn't Monday and I feel up to it. I cough and cough. I make a simply appalling noise. You'd think it was my lungs getting destroyed, not theirs. It sobers them up pretty quickly, I can tell you. Whole bus loads can't stub out fast enough when I get going.

Method number four is a variation on number three. It's just a combination of coughing and glaring. I use it when there's only one smoker left who's pretending my coughing fit is nothing to do with their smoking.

Method number five only works with women. I brush imaginary ash off my clothes. I brush and brush away, eyeing the cigarette, and soon the woman tries holding her fag in a different position. But I just keep on brushing. And 47 in the end she begins to think that, wherever she holds it, her ash is going to float on to my clothing. Defeated, she stubs it out.

Now and then, miraculously, there's a free seat. If it's up the front, I take it. If it's at the back, I ignore it. I'd rather stand. But if it's in the last row between the smokers and the non-smokers, I take it and turn round to start conversations.

'Is that the brand with the coupons that get you the free iron lung?'

'Have you smoked for long?' (That always depresses them. They always have.)

If I've got a snack for my break-time, I start to unwrap it. Then I turn round and say: 'I hope my eating my granola bar isn't going to spoil your cigarette.'

Or I might kneel on the seat, lean over, and chat away merrily.

'We're doing a project on smoking at school. Did you know that there are over a thousand poisons in every cigarette? Did you know that one hundred thousand people every year die earlier than they should because they smoke? Did you know that if you live in the same house as smokers, you get to smoke eighty cigarettes a year without even having one? Did you know . . .'

Everyone at the back of the bus hates me. They all complain about me when they get off.

'That child's a real pain,' they say to the driver. 'She shouldn't be allowed to travel on this bus.'

He passes their sentiments on while I'm standing by his shoulder, waiting for my stop.

'They say you're a nuisance,' he tells me.

'Me?' I say, outraged. '*I'm* the nuisance? I like that!'

'There's not much to choose between you.'

'There most certainly is,' I argue. 'I'll tell you what there is to choose between us. If *they* stopped, *I'd* stop, straight away. If *I* stopped, they'd get *worse*. So I'd choose *me*.'

'None the less,' said the driver, 'I've had more 49

than enough complaints. And until the company changes the rules, smokers are supposed to be welcome on this bus.' (You'll notice he didn't say they *were*. He only said they were *supposed* to be.) 'So, any more trouble from you, young lady, and I put you off at the next corner. Understand?'

Word travels faster than the number 14 bus, I can tell you. By the next morning, everyone knew that I was on probation. I only turned round once, and said quite amiably to the fellow behind me: 'Did you know smokers can get gangrene?' and the bus practically *screeched* to a halt. Before I knew what had happened I was standing on the pavement with my book bag and my gym shoes and my tennis racket and my lunch box and my English folder and my choir music and a huge bag of dress-ups for the class play.

'I did warn you,' said the driver as the automatic doors went 'phut' in my face. 'Don't try to say I didn't warn you.'

I was twenty-five minutes late. Twenty-five minutes! I tried sneaking in the back way, but it was no use because, by the time I crept up the stairs to my classroom, Mrs Phillips had taken the register and marked me absent.

'Twenty-five minutes!' she scolded. 'Absolutely disgraceful. Be late again this week, and you'll be in big trouble.'

I really tried to keep quiet on the bus the next morning. It wasn't my fault I was forced so far down the gangway that I ended up standing over some fat old fellow who could scarcely *breathe*.

He spoke to me first – if you can call it speaking. It was more of a painful wheeze, really. He took his packet out of his pocket, opened it, peeped longingly at all the little killers inside, and closed it up again.

Then he glanced up and saw me watching him.

'Trying to give up,' he explained. 'Doctor's orders.'

Well I had to say *something*, didn't I? I was only being *polite*.

'You can do it!' I encouraged him. 'You can. You can! Fight the good fight! There are eleven million ex-smokers walking around Britain with good clean lungs. You can be the eleven millionth and first!'

That's *all I said*. And it wasn't him who got all shirty. It was the others who sent word up the gangway that I should be put off the bus again — all those not under doctor's orders. Yet.

'Enjoy the walk,' said the driver, pressing the button to shut the bus doors in my face. 'Phut'.

'Bye,' I said.

It wasn't so bad that morning. I only had my book bag and my lunch box and my recorder and my project on Witchcraft and my home-made peephole camera to carry. So I was only twenty minutes late.

'I did warn you,' said Mrs Phillips. 'That's a detention. You're twenty minutes late, so I want you in tomorrow twenty minutes early. You can write me an essay.' She fished about for a title that would do nicely for a punishment. 'I know. *A Business Letter*. And I want it properly set out and neatly written, with perfect spelling.'

I know when I'm beaten. I didn't argue. I just got up twenty minutes earlier the next morning, and caught the bus that comes twenty minutes earlier, and reached school twenty minutes earlier, and sat down to write.

Room 14
Stocklands School
Great Barr Street

21 April

Dear Sir or Madam

I'm writing to tell you how bothered I am that some of the pupils in my class are forced to travel each morning on buses that are so 53 thick with cigarette smoke that they arrive coughing, and with pink eyes. I have the number 14 bus particularly in mind.

In my view, smoking is for kippers, and children should be smokeless zones.

Please ban smoking on single decker buses as soon as possible, particularly the number 14.

Yours faithfully

I left the space at the bottom blank. I didn't sign Mrs Phillips's name in case she thought I was being cheeky.

How was I to know she'd sweep in and scoop it up, read it through, then sign her name with a flourish in the gap I'd left? How was I to know she'd root through the clutter in her desk to find an envelope, and send me off to the office to
54 look up the bus company's address in the

telephone directory? How was I to know she'd even dig in her own purse and give me a stamp?

She saw me looking at her.

'Fight the good fight,' she said.

The reply came a week later. I was surprised to see it was a bit different from the one my mother got back from them last year. There was a lot less of the 'considering the feelings of other passengers' stuff, and a lot more about 'coming to realize the hazards of passive smoking', and 'frequent discussions on the possibility of changing bus company policy in this respect'.

'There you go,' said Mrs Phillips. 'They're half-way to cracking already. Just keep on at 'em.'

And so I do. I'm no trouble at all on the bus now. I've taken to getting up five minutes earlier so I can walk two stops back and catch the bus at the Ferry Lane Factory. (A lot of people get off there, so I get a seat.) I usually sit behind the driver. I look at his *Have a heart* no smoking sign 55 for inspiration, then I dig out one of my four letter pads, and I write my letter.

I write one letter every single morning. (Mum buys the stamps. She says it's all in a good cause.) I write for everyone I know: family, friends, shopkeepers, pen-friends, members of the gym club. Everyone signs their letter. Even Granny and the bus driver signed theirs. Granny says she wouldn't have gone to all the trouble of writing herself, being a smoker; but since I'd bothered it seemed a terrible waste not to post it. The bus driver said it's his bus and he's not allowed to smoke on it, so why should anyone else get away with it? It's not a very lofty attitude, I agree, but I didn't say anything. You see, I'm getting on a lot better with him now, since I started going through the proper channels.

He still thinks I'm weird. But he helps me with my spelling if I get stuck, and he's even taken a couple of my letters home to get his wife 56 and his sister to sign them.

And he lets me know whenever he hears rumours that all the single deckers are going non-smoking. It happens more and more often now. He thinks the change is coming. So do I. In fact, we're so sure that we've worked out which notice we're going to stick on the glass panel behind his seat on the Glorious Day. It's going to say, in big red capital letters:

WARNING
LIGHTING UP ON THIS BUS
CAN SERIOUSLY DAMAGE
YOUR HEALTH

I'll stop fighting the good fight then. But, if you see the number 14 going by, you'll still be able to recognize me. I'll be the one staring idly out of the window.